PET OWNER'S GUIDE TO THE
LOVEBIRD

Alexander James

RINGPRESS

Photography: Keith Allison

Published by Ringpress Books Limited,
PO Box 8, Lydney, Gloucestershire,
GL15 4YN, United Kingdom.

First published 1999

ISBN 1 86054 126 7

Printed and bound in Hong Kong by Printworks International

CONTENTS

CARING FOR LOVEBIRDS

5

Dangers; Feeding lovebirds; Balanced diet; Seeds; Seed ratios; Soaked seeds; Green foods; Other foods; Junk foods; Grit and minerals: Supplements; Feeding method; New items; Routine care (Wing clipping; Cleaning;) Observation; Outdoors; Handling; Training.

BREEDING

6

Be prepared; Nestboxes; Nesting material; Initial stock; Sexing; Breeding age; Breeding facts; Problems; Leg rings; Exhibition.

HEALTH CARE

7

General strategy; Know your birds: Signs of ill health (Physical signs; Abnormal behaviour); Assess the situation; What to do; Treatments; Wounds or breaks.

1 *Introducing Lovebirds*

Lovebirds are more popular today than at any time in their long and (at times) chequered history. Indeed, only the budgerigar and the cockatiel enjoy greater popularity. There are many reasons why lovebirds have won their way into the hearts of breeders, exhibitors and pet owners alike. Their small size – they are among the smallest of all parrots – has obvious appeal to those unable to own the larger members of the parrot family.

Their colourful and immaculate plumage is another asset, while the numerous colour mutations that have appeared over the years have

Small in size, and beautiful to look at, the lovebird has become increasingly popular as a pet bird.

attracted many to become devotees. However, in spite of their considerable popularity as a group, certain species still represent an enormous challenge to breeders.

Further, lovebirds are not always the charming creatures their name would suggest. Indeed, within mixed collection aviaries they can become a real menace, their aggressive nature belying their diminutive size. As pets, many owners find they are not quite what they expected. This is invariably because the owner did not devote enough time to seeking information about them beforehand.

This book will provide any potential owner with the basic information needed to select, house and care for these interesting pint-sized parrots, whether for cage or aviary, breeding or exhibition.

PARROTS

The term 'parrot' is applicable to about 330 birds that share a believed common evolutionary path. They may differ considerably in size, and yet are readily distinguished from other bird groups when a number of features are collectively observed – in particular, the beak, plumage and feet.

The beak is hooked, yet is not so curved, nor so long, as in the raptors (birds of prey). The lower mandible is usually proportionately larger than in the raptors. In parrots, the beak is used as a third foot when climbing.

In many species, the plumage is colourful. Red, blue, green and yellow in many hues and patterns are common, but there are also a number of species that are sober, being predominantly brown or green.

The feet are termed 'zygodactyl', meaning two toes facing forward and two backwards, whereas in raptors, three face forward and one backwards. Parrots are very able in the use of their feet, holding and turning even very small seeds.

A number of parrots are famed for their ability to mimic sounds, including those of mammals, other birds, and the human voice – thus the term 'learning parrot-fashion'. Lovebirds are not among these. Any person hoping to teach their lovebird to talk or to whistle tunes will be disappointed, which is not to say they cannot be taught a few words.

The habit of sitting close together in pairs gave the lovebird its name.

CLASSIFICATION

All life forms are classified by zoologists into a system of hierarchically arranged groups. The advantage of this system is that it allows entire collections of species, such as the parrots, the bears or the apes to be discussed without the need to name all the members comprising that group. At the top of this assemblage is the kingdom Animalia, which contains all animals.

The kingdom is divided into a number of groups based on shared features. These groups are divided into further groups. This eventually results in collections of life forms that are similar in most of their features – these are the species.

All birds are classified in a major group called Aves. This is divided into groups, known as orders. The one containing the parrots is called Psittaciformes – the parrot-like birds. This is divided into three families. One contains the cockatoos (which includes the popular cockatiel), one the lories, which are primarily nectar feeders, and the final group contains the so-called 'true parrots'. This has the name Psittacidae: it contains most of the parrots, including our subject, the lovebirds.

GENUS

The psittacids are divided into groups called genera (sing. genus). The genus housing the lovebirds is named *Agapornis*, which is Greek for birds of love, so called because of their habit of sitting close together in pairs. The French common name for these birds is 'Inséparables', which conveys much the same meaning.

The genus is divided into a number of groups that form freely-breeding populations of individuals. Such individuals are called species. They are identified by giving them a name which, when used in association with the genus, creates a binomial that is unique within the animal kingdom – no two life forms can have the same species name.

There are nine recognised lovebird species. These are discussed in the following chapter. Eight are native to Africa, one to the island of Madagascar. The only acceptable group below a species in formal classification is a subspecies. These are identified by having a trinomial. You may note that the genus and species names are placed into a typeface that differs from the main text. It is normally in italic. This applies only to the genus, species and subspecies names, never to a rank above the genus.

EARLY HISTORY

It is unknown when lovebirds were first introduced to Europe. They were certainly not among the first parrots to be kept. That distinction probably rests with the parakeets of Asia which were sent to Macedonia (Greece) by Alexander the Great during his epic travels.

The Romans were known to keep many African parrot species, but not until the 18th century can any records be found that suggest lovebirds were known to Europeans. This means that only the many Australian species have a shorter avicultural history than the lovebirds. Ironically, the first few lovebird species to be recorded in Europe have proved to be the most difficult to maintain. These are the Red-faced, the Madagascar and the Abyssinian.

The first of the lovebirds to be classified scientifically was the Red-faced in 1758, followed by the Madagascar some thirty years later. The last species to be officially recognised was the Black-cheeked, in 1906.

Aviculture (the keeping and rearing of birds), as a popular hobby, blossomed during the later years of the 19th century. As a consequence, many thousands of lovebirds were shipped to Europe. Most failed to survive, due to the rigours of the journey and lack of knowledge of their dietary and nesting requirements. Breeders quickly lost interest in this group – after all, the budgerigar was the boom species and was becoming

Many thousands of lovebirds perished on the journey to Europe when they were transported from their native African home.

more and more valuable. There was little incentive to keep cantankerous pocket-sized parrots, such as lovebirds. Even so, some breeders persevered, and the Peach-faced lovebird displayed a willingness to breed if given reasonable facilities.

CHANGING TIMES

As the 20th century got underway, the arrival of the Masked, Nyasa and Fischer's injected new interest in this group, the more so because they proved to be willing breeders. Unfortunately, the 1930 parrot ban in Britain meant that species not already established would sooner or later become scarce if the ban persisted. It did so for 22 years, and was then lifted for only a short

time before further restrictions were applied.

By the end of the Second World War, lovebirds had largely faded from the avicultural scene in Britain, other than in a few collections. But, as the bird hobby once again emerged from wartime chaos, so interest was rekindled in the lovebirds. However, few people kept them as cage pets, so the main market was for aviary and exhibition purposes. In fact, it was the exhibitor breeders who can largely be thanked for maintaining and establishing the presently available species of these beautiful birds.

The pet lovebird became the forte of Americans, and, to a lesser extent, of Australians, both of whom saw qualities in these birds largely overlooked by Europeans. The Europeans' pet needs were invariably met by the larger parrots of Africa and South America, with Asian species being lower-cost alternatives.

PARROT BANS

During the 1960s, the effect of the 1959 Australian ban on exporting its fauna was being felt throughout the avicultural world. It was the writing on the wall for any breeder who could look further than the immediate future. Clearly, other countries would follow the Australian example, and they did. This would mean that formerly inexpensive species that were not well established in aviaries would slowly vanish.

The challenge was to establish breeding populations that would have higher values, as imports became more scarce and more costly. More lovebirds were bred, increasing the potential for mutations to appear, which they did. In turn, these created more interest in lovebirds as exhibition prospects, and also as pets. And so we arrive where we began this chapter, with the lovebirds having overcome many obstacles to

Careful thought must be given before taking on the responsibility of owning lovebirds.

establish themselves as one of the most popular of all parrot groups.

OWNING LOVEBIRDS

Although the idea of owning a lovebird may be as appealing, they should not be obtained without very careful consideration of their nature. Just as important are the potential owner's personality, and the environment in which the lovebird will be living. If these factors are not fully appreciated the chances of a mismatch will increase dramatically, and disappointment will be the result. These comments are especially applicable to pet owners, who are, and should be, looking for a one-to-one relationship with the animal they wish to own. For aviary owners, an understanding of lovebird traits may avoid problems within mixed or colony collection situations. As a guide, a lovebird can be expected to live for ten years, sometimes more.

PET LOVEBIRDS

Whereas even adult budgerigars and cockatiels not familiar with being handled can be quickly finger-tamed and become excellent pets, this is normally not true with lovebirds. To become easily handled they must be obtained as soon as they are feeding independently. Ideally, hand-reared individuals are the ones to own – they will already be used to humans.

Such birds are playful, lively, hardy and very companionable, unlike those not handled a lot as babies. These will be aloof, nervous and very quick to nip. Indeed, even a very tame lovebird may nip.

Many pet owners, seeing a pair of lovebirds huddled together in a pet shop, will purchase a pair. This is fine, but it must be appreciated that both will be far less inclined to want to form any sort of close bond with their owner. But, if the owner does not have lots of time to devote to a single bird, it would be better to obtain a pair because they do, like most birds, enjoy having a companion.

I will go further. If a potential pet owner does not have lots of time, lots of patience, and no fear of the occasional hard nip, then the lovebird is not the best parrot to own. The fact that these birds are relatively inexpensive does not mean they make ideal pets. Lovebirds are a challenge, more so than any other popular parrot. Once bonded with their owners, they are every bit as good as any

An aviary provides the ideal environment.

parrot, and have that great advantage – they are small. They are more agile than budgies or cockatiels, and will enthral their owners with their antics.

AVIARY LOVEBIRDS

The safest way to keep lovebirds in an aviary situation is in pairs. You will see these birds in mixed collection aviaries, but the owner is taking a gamble, much as would be the case with lovebirds kept in a colony system. Beginners often wonder why birds that live in flocks in the wild cannot live in harmony when in aviaries. The answer lies in the fact that all birds are territorial. They become even more so during the breeding season.

Most lovebirds are especially pugnacious and will not shrink from attacking even larger birds.

They can inflict serious wounds on smaller birds, and will not hesitate to kill the offspring of other species sharing the same aviary. Indeed, they will often show the same aggression to their own kind in colony situations. The first keys to successfully keeping lovebirds with other species, or in colonies, lie in the size of the aviary and the number of residents.

If you already have an aviary and are thinking of adding one or two lovebirds, the best advice is not to, unless the aviary is very large and there are no timid and small residents. It should be added that lovebirds are by no means the only species that display aggression in mixed collections. This fact is true of many species, and of all species during breeding periods when nestboxes are in place.

2 Lovebird Species

From the hobbyist's perspective, lovebirds can be divided into three groups. One is the sexually dimorphic group (meaning that the sexes can be identified by their appearance), which contains three species. Another is termed the white eye-ringed group, which contains four species. The third group is the intermediate, containing two species that are intermediate between the dimorphic and the white eye-ringed groups.

Of the nine species, three can be regarded as readily available, one is never seen in the hobby, and the remaining five range from uncommon to rare. What must be appreciated about aviculture is that things can, and do, change over any span of time. For this reason all nine species are described in this chapter, because what is uncommon or rare today could become quite common in a few years.

The only unlikelihood is that Swindern's lovebird will ever become available, let alone popular, in the foreseeable future. It has virtually no record at all in captivity, but is included for completeness – no one can say for sure what the future might hold.

GROUP MEMBERS

SEXUALLY DIMORPHIC: Red-faced (very rare); Madagascar (very rare, but once quite common and low-cost); Abyssinian (uncommon, but still available).

WHITE EYE-RINGED: Masked (common and readily available); Fischer's (common and readily available); Black-cheeked (formerly common, now less so); Nyasa (rare).

INTERMEDIATE: Peach-faced (the most popular species, readily

An aviary show is the place to see a variety of species, and there will be experts on hand to give you advice.

available); Swindern's (has never been available in aviculture).

PURCHASE COST

Colour mutational forms are more costly, depending on how difficult they are to produce, or how new they are. Quality breeding birds, especially young proven pairs, together with exhibition standard lovebirds, will of course be even more costly.

SPECIES GUIDE

The following species descriptions are arranged on the basis of the most popular species, followed by the less commonly seen, the rare species, and finally the single unavailable species. The common

name is followed by the scientific one, the person who first described the species, and the date when this was first published. In all instances the original authors of the names did not place them in their present genus (indicated by placing the name in brackets).

PEACH-FACED *Agapornis roseicollis* (Vieillot) 1817
Synonym: Rosy-faced.
Distribution: South-western Africa, especially Angola. Length: 15 cm (6 in). Sexes: Similar. Beak: Horn coloured. Legs: Grey. Irides: Brown.

The face, crown and throat are rose pink. There is a very thin white eye-ring, but not comparable to that of the white eye-ringed group. Body and neck are a light apple green. The wings are a darker green, while the primary feathers are very dark green and edged in yellow-green. The rump is blue.

The Peach-faced is the most readily available species and has always proved a reliable breeder. It is also the most aggressive of the popular lovebirds when in mixed collections, or when attempts are made to colony breed. It may even prove quarrelsome with its own mate out of the breeding season. It is also the noisiest species, but in outdoor aviaries this is nothing like as obvious as when it is indoors.

Its negative aspects aside, its popularity is well deserved because it makes a very handsome exhibition bird. There are more

The Peach-faced variety is the most readily available – and the most noisy!

mutations established for this species than for any other lovebird. These include the lutino, marine (formerly termed pastel blue), cinnamon, silver, lacewing, violet, jade, olive, cobalt, yellow, golden cherry, orange-faced and pied. In combination, the potential permutations are legion.

It should be stated that, while some mutational colours are very impressive (the lutino, American silver and Japanese cherry, for example), others sound better than they actually look. Further, some breeders apply fanciful names to permutations and these create much confusion in the hobby.

MASKED *Agapornis personata* (Reichenow) 1887
Synonyms: Yellow-collared, Black-masked. Distribution: North-eastern Tanzania. Length: 14.6 cm (5.75 in). Sexes: Similar. Beak: Red. Legs: Grey. Irides: Brown.

As suggested by its name, the head of this species is black to dark brown, covering the head in the manner of a hood. The naked eye-ring skin is white. The breast and neck are yellow, often with an orange hue. The rest of the body is light green. The wings are dark green and the rump is grey-blue.

This species, while not as prolific as the Peach-faced, is still prolific and very hardy, and is thus suited to novices. It is less aggressive than the Peach-faced.

Many breeders have established small colonies under aviary or flight conditions, and it is often seen in mixed collections.

However, it is a lovebird, so you never know when one or more may suddenly decide to display the belligerent side of their nature. It is therefore best kept in pairs. They make fine pets.

A number of mutations are established, of which the blue is the most popular – and a very beautiful bird it is. Although called the blue Masked, the mask itself is still black – 'blue' refers to the body colour. The yellow of the breast and neck becomes off-white, while the beak colour is diluted. Other popular mutations are the lutino, albino, violet, yellow, white, and pied.

FISCHER'S *Agapornis fischeri* (Reichenow) 1887
Synonyms: None. Distribution: North-western Tanzania, south and south-east of Lake Victoria. Length: 14 cm (5.5 in). Sexes: Similar. Beak: Red. Legs: Grey. Irides: Brown.

The entire head is a fiery orange

The Lutino Peach-faced lovebird is a striking colour mutation.

that extends down the neck and the breast. Body and wings are green, with some yellow on the underbelly and tail feathers. The rump is blue. The white eye-ring is, as in each of this group, very apparent.

This species has always been a popular lovebird and is a well-established breeder. It is not as plentiful as the lovebirds previously discussed. This is not due to any unwillingness on the part of the species to reproduce, but reflects its lesser popularity, which also accounts for its higher price.

Mutational forms include the beautiful blue, the lutino, the yellow, sea green, pied, spangled and other more rare varieties. These will ensure that the future for this species continues to be progressive.

BLACK-CHEEKED *Agapornis nigrigenis* (Sclater) 1906
Synonym: Black-faced.
Distribution: Zambia. Length: 14 cm (5.5 in). Sexes: Similar. Beak: Red. Legs: Grey. Irides: Yellowish to brown.

This species looks somewhat similar to the Nyasa and the Masked, but with a much reduced dark area on the head than in the latter species. This is black only on the cheeks, becoming brown on the forehead and crown. The white eye-ring immediately tells you it is a member of this group of lovebirds. The breast is green with some yellow, rather than yellow as in the Masked. The throat has a salmon-orange suffusion. The green wings are a darker shade than in the Nyasa.

The Black-cheeked is nothing like as commonly available as the three species already discussed. This was not always the case, for there was a time when it was exported from its small distribution range in the thousands. It proved a willing breeder, but the opportunity to establish viable populations was missed due to its low cost. This eventually resulted in its demise, and in many breeders hybridising it with others of the white eye-ringed group.

The Black-cheeked, if of pure strain (which would be hard to find), is a delightful lovebird. It is less aggressive than the more popular species and has been successfully bred on a colony basis. There are no known mutations, though these have been introduced by hybridisation.

NYASA *Agapornis lilianae* (Shelley) 1894
Synonyms: Lilian's, Nyasaland.
Distribution: Zambia, Malawi,

The delicate plumage of the pastel Peach-faced variety.

Zimbabwe. Length: 13 cm (5 in). Sexes: Similar. Beak: Red. Legs: Grey. Irides: Yellowish to Brown.

The Nyasa is similar to the Black-cheeked, but the head is red, as in Fischer's, though paler and less extensive, and is restricted to an area from the back of the neck to the throat. The green of the body and wings is a lighter shade than is seen in the Black-cheeked. The white eye-ring is present, and the beak is rather smaller than in the previously discussed species.

The blue-masked lovebird is the most popular of the colour mutations within this species.

It is unfortunate that this little lovebird never maintained its former popularity, for it has much to commend it. It has bred well on a colony basis and will coexist with other small birds in a mixed collection without being the rogue most species are (although there are always exceptions).

It displays far less inclination to nip, so is an excellent pet prospect, and is quieter than the other species. A lutino mutation has been established for many years, and other mutations have been transferred to the species via hybridisation.

ABYSSINIAN *Agapornis taranta* (Stanley) 1814
Synonym: Black-winged.
Distribution: Central and eastern Ethiopia, also southern Eritrea.
Length: 16.5 cm (6.5 in). Sexes: Dimorphic. Beak: Red. Legs: Grey. Irides: Brown.

The sexes are easily distinguished because the cock has bright red on its forehead, the colour extending to the eyes, which are encircled in red. Females lack the red. The rest of the body is green with a dark band across the tail feathers.

The Abyssinian has never been a

The Masked lovebird tends to be less aggressive than the Peach-faced variety.

popular lovebird. Its belligerent nature, added to its size – the largest of the lovebirds – makes it unsuitable for anything but pair breeding.

It is a quiet species, but will probably never become popular, because it is not readily available and also because it is less willing to breed than are the others so far discussed.

RED-FACED *Agapornis pullaria* (Linnaeus) 1758
Synonyms: None. Distribution: Western equatorial Africa to central Africa and south to northern Angola. Length: 15 cm (6 in). Sexes: Dimorphic. Beak: Red. Legs: Grey. Irides: Brown.

This species is similar to the Abyssinian in colour, though smaller and with more red on the face, which extends to form a half circle under the throat. However, females also have red faces, but they are much paler. They also have green under-wing coverts, and the edge of the wing is yellowish – in males, these areas are black.

The Red-faced has never been a popular lovebird because it was always a difficult species to breed. Its wild nesting site is within large termite mounds, and creating suitable alternatives proved all but impossible for many years. They are now bred in captivity, but are a nervous species. They are the most gregarious of all lovebirds and can safely be bred in colonies with minimal problems. Lutino and blue mutations have been established, but are rare.

MADAGASCAR *Agapornis cana* (Gmelin) 1788
Synonyms: Grey-headed, Lavender-headed. Distribution: Island of Madagascar; introduced to Comoro Isles, Mauritius, Mafia and Zanzibar, which lie east of the African coast. Length: 14 cm (5.5 in). Sexes: Dimorphic. Beak: White-grey. Legs: Grey. Irides: Brown.

This species, in its male form, is quite imposing. The entire head, throat, chest and neck are a light grey, the rest of the body being green. The female lacks the grey, which is replaced by a mottled sort of green, especially on the crown and neck.

Although once available in considerable numbers, this has not been the case for many years, and the species is rare. It requires a large aviary and lots of solitude if breeding is to be attempted. The female is very aggressive out of season with any other birds, so pairs are the rule. A pied mutation has appeared, but is rare.

SWINDERN'S *Agapornis swinderniana* (Kuhl) 1820
Synonyms: Black-collared, Liberian. Distribution: Liberia and Cameroon to Zaire. Length: 13.5 cm (5.25 in). Sexes: Similar. Beak: Black. Legs: Dark Grey. Irides: Yellow-brown.

The rarest of all lovebirds, Swindern's is unusual in that it has a black beak. A thin black band encircles the base of its neck, followed by a yellow band, while the rest of the bird is green, darker on the wings than on the body.

There is no record of this species being kept in Western aviculture. Attempts to maintain it in African aviaries have all failed due to its specialised fresh fig diet. It is very much a bird of the dense equatorial forests. Other than its rarity value, I doubt Swindern's would ever be a popular bird were it available in numbers because the other species are more attractive and this, ultimately, determines popularity.

3 Choosing Lovebirds

Before purchasing lovebirds, it is very important that potential owners do as much as they can to ensure they will get the right bird(s) for their needs, be this as a pet, for breeding, or for exhibition. The biggest mistake beginners make is to be impatient and to rush into this.

It can prove a disastrous error with lovebirds. The result may well be a totally unsuitable pet, a poor breeding bird or an exhibition prospect that will have little chance of ever being a success on the show bench. It would indeed be a wonderful world if all people selling things were totally honest. Alas, this is not always the case. It is up to the buyer to beware and to know how they can sort out the genuine from those best avoided. It must also be kept in mind that some sellers are not necessarily dishonest, but more concerned to sell what they have rather than to provide what the buyer actually wants. The following is a list of the key aspects of buying a lovebird; each is then examined in turn.

- Decide what role the bird is expected to play (pet, breeding or exhibition).
- Decide on the species and colour wanted.
- Be sure to view a number of suppliers (and magazines) so a typical price can be established.
- Compare like with like.
- Take special note of the conditions the birds are kept under.
- Note whether all the birds on view are healthy, not just those you are interested in.
- Inspect the bird.

THE BIRD'S ROLE
If a lovebird is required as a pet, it must be obtained when very young. The ideal bird will have

been hand-reared. It will have no fear of humans, will be finger-tame and weaned on to a balanced seed and mixed vegetable and fruit diet. The only other option is a youngster that has very recently left the nest and has ideally been finger-tamed. Such a bird will be six to ten weeks old.

If a lovebird remains more than a few weeks in a stock cage or aviary without interacting with humans, it will be much harder to make into the perfect pet. It can still be done, but requires considerable patience. A person with such patience will get the best out of these birds, and so is actually the very one who should obtain the ideal individual in the first place. You will have to gamble on what sex you get, because youngsters look alike in all species – but either sex will make a good pet.

The potential breeder may purchase quality youngsters or proven adults. A novice breeder needs to know as much as possible about the birds they start with. This means age, genotype (the bird's genetic constitution), especially in colour mutations, past breeding record (if any) and what the general standard of the breeder's stock is like.

The exhibitor requires young birds that are of good type, with no missing toes or claws, good colour and markings, and which are very steady in their temperament. A nervous bird will not make a good show bird.

SPECIES AND COLOUR

Most pet owners will normally choose from one of the three most popular species, and often like to own one of the mutational colours. However, you should remember that the less readily available species have excellent track records as pets because a few of them have more gentle dispositions than the most popular species. But they cost more and will be more difficult to locate.

Once you have decided on the species and colour, you should not let a seller talk you out of this just because they do not have one. Nor should you accept a less than ideal bird just because it is the species and colour you want, and is convenient to obtain. In these circumstances, a good and fit example of another species would be the better choice.

From a breeder's perspective, there are many ways to view which species is best to have if you are keen on lovebirds and are

The novice bird-keeper should start with one of the popular species, like these Masked lovebirds, in order to gain experience.

happy to take any species and colour. The very popular birds will be easiest to obtain and less costly. But it costs as much to feed them as is does those that command better prices.

My advice would be to start with one of the three popular species so that you can gain experience. During this time, study the more rare species with the plan to obtain these once you are satisfied you intend to remain a breeder. In the long run, it is probable that a small stud of the rarer birds will be more cost-efficient, providing the breeder takes an active interest in exhibitions, which is discussed in a later chapter.

SUPPLIERS

You are recommended never to purchase a lovebird 'sight unseen', unless it comes from a breeder with the highest of reputations. It carries too many unnecessary risks. Always visit the supplier so that you can view the premises and their stock. There are only two worthwhile sources of lovebirds – a good pet store and a reputable breeder. Visit a number, so you can establish what is a typical price for the species and colour you want.

Living conditions should be light and airy, with a high standard of cleanliness and hygiene.

You should also purchase one or more of the avicultural magazines on sale at newsagents. These will contain lovebird adverts, often quoting prices. It is also very worthwhile visiting one or more foreign bird shows. At these you will see many lovebirds, and meet breeders happy to discuss the pros and cons of the various species.

LIKE WITH LIKE

When comparing prices, always compare like with like. A common error for beginners is to compare price with price, meaning this lovebird is more costly than the one elsewhere, so we will buy the cheaper one. The least expensive lovebirds of any species or mutation will be the least desirable. They represent the ones most cheaply bred and reared, and the ones that have received the least attention. From these, all others start to rise in cost, depending what 'extras' they have – rather like a car.

These extras are the quality of the bird – its breeding and conformation; age; and the way it was reared – meaning whether it has been hand-fed or given much attention. Do not expect to buy a little gem of a lovebird for the same price as you would pay a backyard breeder or dealer selling inferior stock maintained under equally inferior conditions. Of course, you would not do that, would you? But many thousands do, and learn the hard way.

LIVING CONDITIONS

When first visiting a supplier, take special note of the general conditions of the premises, and then of those the birds are living under. Unless they are both of high standard, you should make a hasty retreat. Any person involved with selling birds has no excuse for dirtiness, untidy, crowded or otherwise unsuitable living conditions. They should not be selling birds. The risk of illness rises dramatically, and it displays an uncaring attitude. Only support those pet stores and breeders who clearly maintain daily standards of hygiene and consideration for their stock. This does not mean they must all have state-of-the-art operations; it means that what they have is up to minimal standards. These are:

- Light and airy conditions, with satisfactory ventilation.
- Floor and walls are clean, and not dingy and in need of attention. They should be of a surface easily kept in a clean state.
- No unpleasant smell that suggests lack of cleaning.
- No open bags of seed and other foods scattered about, which are easily fouled by various means.
- The seller displays sound personal hygiene in wearing a nylon overall or other clean clothing.
- There must never be bags of cage rubbish left near the birds. In the case of a breeding stud, the immediate

Check out all the birds in the aviary rather than focusing all your attention on the one you want to purchase.

area around the aviaries or bird room should not contain piles of rubbish or rotting vegetation.

With respect to the cages, observe that:

- All surfaces are clean, with no areas of damaged, rusted material that represent an obvious health hazard.
- Perches should be clean and not worn to the point where they are clearly in need of replacement.
- Food and water vessels should be clean, and neither chipped nor cracked. They should also contain seed/water, and not be empty or nearly so.
- Floors should be clean and not caked with faecal matter that has not been removed for days.
- Birds should not be so crowded they have no option but to sit tightly together on perches.

● Lovebirds should not be sharing cages with any other species. This represents very bad management.

BIRD HEALTH

Many novices tend to focus their attention on the birds they are interested in, taking little time to study other birds in the same establishment. But these other birds may be unwell. Sooner or later their problem will affect all the birds, which may not display the signs until days after they have been purchased. The signs of ill

health are discussed in the health care chapter.

Obviously, especially in a large establishment, a bird may suddenly display ill health that goes unnoticed for a short time (but never more than a few hours) before the seller sees it. But, if a number of birds clearly look unwell, you are advised to find another supplier.

If you are told that the bird only has a minor chill, or other problem which will clear up within 24 hours, tell the seller you will come back after that time. You are paying for a healthy bird, not one that could be very sickly within a few days. It is the seller's problem – do not let it become yours, as many a pet owner does.

PHYSICAL INSPECTION
If you are happy with the seller, a physical inspection of the bird you like should not be necessary, but if you are selecting potential breeding stock or for exhibition, it may be prudent. Check closely the alignment of the beak, the feathers of the wings, and the toes of the feet. You should also gently feel the flesh on either side of the

If you are seeking breeding and show stock, there are important factors to consider when making your choice.

The bird you select should be bright-eyed, clean and healthy, with an alert, inquisitive manner.

sternum keel (the breastbone) to ensure it is not hollow, a condition known as 'going light'. It often indicates a nutritional deficiency. If the bird is hand-reared, it will have no problems perching on your finger.

When visiting a breeder's aviaries, view a number of birds so you can be satisfied that the general standard of quality is good. By visiting shows and a number of breeders, you will develop a better image of quality than if you go to visit just one aviary or pet store. If the breeder is also an exhibitor, they will no doubt be happy to show you trophies or cards and some of the birds that won them.

If the advice is this chapter is carefully implemented, it will not guarantee you the ideal bird (no one can do that), but it will greatly reduce the potential of your being sold a bad one. You will at least start with an excellent prospect; whether it achieves its potential will be very much down to how you care for and interact with it.

4 Setting Up Home

One of the considerable advantages of lovebirds is that they can be housed in cages that would be too small for most parrots. Likewise, lovebird aviaries can be of smaller dimensions than for many other species. Also, lovebirds are not noisy. They are unlikely to upset the neighbours with the high-pitched and raucous screeching that even some small parrots are capable of.

CAGE FIRST
You should always purchase a bird's housing ahead of the bird itself – never at the same time. There are two sound reasons for this. Firstly, it gives you the opportunity to view many cage styles in different stores so you can find the one you like best. You may even have to put in a special order for it. It also enables you to begin viewing lovebirds, thus not rushing this vital process.

If you purchase the bird and cage on the same day, everything becomes hurried. This is never the best way to start. Once you obtain the desired cage it can be tried in a few locations, then set up complete with furnishings. Now you have the time to decide on the bird, knowing this is all you need think about because its home is waiting.

CAGE SIZE
Any cage large enough for a budgerigar will accommodate a lovebird. This said, and if you want your bird to be very happy, think in terms of a much larger home for it. It will provide more room for worthwhile furnishings, and room for the pet to play. Some of the modern designs are very attractive, making them nice furniture pieces in themselves.

A worthwhile cage will cost quite a bit more than the pet itself. Such an investment is recommended from every practical viewpoint. You will find there are many fanciful designs in pet shops, usually at the lower end of the price range. They are invariably designed and produced by companies without any real knowledge of birds. Their object is to produce a cage at the lowest cost which will appeal to inexperienced pet owners. Beware that what may look attractive to you may be a very poor home for your lovebird.

The most important factor in the design of a cage is usable flying space. Tall cylindrical cages, pagoda or Victorian styles waste a lot of space. You cannot beat a simple square or rectangle shape.

FEATURES
A well-designed cage will contain

Lovebirds can be kept in a cage, but it must be as spacious as possible.

a number of features, the number depending on its cost. Make a note of these. When you shop, compare the cages against your list.

Large access door with safe locking mechanism: The larger the door, the better for attending to cleaning chores, and also for getting your hand in when you want to remove the pet physically.

Complete side opening: In the more costly units, an entire cage side will open to provide complete access. It is invariably designed to double as a large landing and play area. It may also contain a regular door within it, so you have flexible options. Another variation is that the roof may additionally open to create a landing/play area.

Pull-out tray: All cages should feature this, though some of the low cost models have a plastic removable base that clips on to the wire of the cage – these are best avoided.

An extra feature of some cages is that they contain a false wire floor, through which debris and uneaten food fall to the tray below. This is an unnecessary feature with no realistic advantages. The wire floor is not good for the bird's feet, and becomes clotted with faecal matter. Useful food items are wasted that would ordinarily be eaten from the floor. Owners may also be encouraged to be less than diligent in cleaning the tray beneath false floors, because the bird is not walking on the accumulated debris. This then increases the health risk factor. Birds enjoy pecking over a solid floor, which is a very natural thing for them to do.

Side tidies: The more upmarket cages will feature angled perimeter slats just above the base. These catch most (though not all) seeds, fruits and feathers that may fall out of the cage when the bird is eating while clinging on to the cage bars. The debris is channelled back to the sliding base tray.

Legs and castors: Large cages come complete with legs and/or castors. The latter are especially useful for relocating the cage to clean under it.

Food and water containers: There is a vast range of styles and qualities in these items. Here we are concerned with the way they are featured in the cage. Gravity-

A gravity-fed water-bottle can be attached to the cage or aviary.

Perches: Low-cost cages may feature plastic perches. These are best removed and replaced with either dowelling or natural wooden perches. Plastic can create sores on the feet of birds; many birds simply do not like them at all. The ideal perch will have a variable thickness along its length. This provides excellent exercise for the toes and reduces the risk of sores. Lovebirds will strip natural perches of their bark (which is nutritious), and so they must be replaced on a regular basis.

Other features: Inexpensive cages may have sharp metal projections on them. The quality of the chrome or epoxy coating may only give limited wear before it rusts or is removed. The distance between cage bars should not exceed 190 mm (0.75 in).

fed water-bottles are the simplest way of providing a supply of fresh water.

Food containers may simply be plastic or metal hang-on types that can be placed anywhere in the cage, or the type that can be filled from the outside without the need to open the cage door. The latter is the most practical. Seed vessels are discussed in Chapter Five: Caring For Lovebirds.

FURNISHINGS
You will need a suitable covering for the floor of your cage. This can be one of four types. A sandsheet, loose sand, biodegradable natural floor litter (as used for cats) or unprinted paper (the ink on newsprint can be dangerous). Do not use sawdust or cedar and similar pine shavings – they are very dangerous

A number of perches of varying width are required.

to your lovebird's health.

If sand is used, ensure it is a generous layer – most owners make this too thin. If paper is used, insert a few sheets and remove and replace these one or two at a time each day. Do not use silicone cat litter – only the quality, natural fibre types.

A very beneficial furnishing is a birdbath. In a large cage it may be featured internally, or it may be the clip-on type in a small cage, which fits on to the open cage door. Within an indoor flight, it can be a heavy shallow, earthenware pot containing a depth of 2.5 cm (1 in) of water. Lovebirds enjoy bathing. It is beneficial for their feather condition, especially during moulting periods. These are often year-round, and called a 'soft moult' under indoor conditions.

The range of toys is bewildering. Many are low-cost and nothing more than plastic junk. The problem they often create is that pet owners, in the desire to keep their pet happy, will unduly crowd the cage with these, so it becomes a veritable maze. This temptation should be avoided like the plague. The smaller the cage, the fewer toys it should contain. They take up far more important fluttering/flying space than they provide in healthy entertainment. When a lovebird is seen to be constantly playing with one or two toys, it is not because it especially enjoys them. More likely, it is bored to death! It focuses on the toys in an effort to relieve its boredom.

Useful toys include lengths of climbing rope, sturdy ladders, strong hoops, frameworks that can be climbed in and out of, and natural items such as wooden thread bobbins and twigs (especially good). The plastic rocking toys, balls, mirrors, revolving ladders and their like are the forte of owners whose birds basically have insufficient space in which to indulge in more wholesome and natural activities such as climbing, chewing and fluttering/flying.

INDOOR FLIGHTS

If space and cost permit, you cannot beat an indoor flight, especially if you are unable to spend as much time as you would like with your lovebirds. You can obtain these from all good pet and avicultural outlets, in a wide range of sizes and a variety of costs. Be sure they feature castors so that they are easily moved from one place to another. A flight affords so much more potential for natural furnishing, and the birds will benefit from all that extra space – enough to actually fly in.

CAGE LOCATION

It is crucial that a lovebird's cage is sited in a healthy and strategic position. It must never be subjected to direct sunlight that the bird cannot escape from – in front of windows, for example. This creates excessive heat and rapid temperature fluctuations that are always unhealthy for birds. These are also created when the cage faces an outside door that enables cold draughts to enter the cage. Likewise, on top of, in front of, or adjacent to heating or cooling units and fans is not a good idea.

In terms of height, the need is such that when the lovebird is

Lovebirds rely on each other for company, and although some toys are appreciated, it is better not to overcrowd the cage or aviary.

perched, this roughly corresponds to your eye level. A low position intimidates the bird and makes chores harder. Additionally, a pet likes to see what is going on around it in a room. The cage should not be placed on tables or similar if pets like cats are present. They will delight in trying to claw the bird, and their presence close to the cage will frighten and stress it. Another consideration is that,

if there is a wall behind the cage, your bird will appreciate it because it will provide a sense of security. It can retreat to the wall end if it is suddenly frightened.

The best room in which to locate the cage is the one you spend most time in, as long as this is not the kitchen. This is full of dangerous fumes and health hazards, especially when the pet is allowed out of its cage.

AVIARIES

Discussion of aviaries in an introductory book is not possible in the depth needed. What follows is a basic primer – more detailed works should be consulted. Lovebirds are excellent aviary subjects, being colourful, easy to breed (the popular species) and hardy. They are able to withstand typical temperate winters as long as a well-insulated shelter is available to them. However, some owners deny them access to outdoor flights during the coldest periods, or overnight, and provide some background overnight heat in the shelter.

A lovebird aviary need not be especially large, which means a number of pairs can be kept in the most modest of gardens. The typical aviary will contain a flight of 1.5 m (5 ft) or more, and a width of 0.9 m (3 ft) or more (the larger the better, especially in terms of length).

At the end of the flight will be

An outdoor aviary fitted with nestboxes.

An aviary cannot be planted because lovebirds will destroy the vegetation, but perches with foliage can be provided.

the shelter, into which the birds will go to feed and to roost for the night. This is usually in the form of a bird room that contains the shelters and has a working area with cupboards for the owner's convenience in attending to chores. It is always better if the bird room has the benefit of utilities – electricity, water and sewage, and an access door to the flight from the outside. This should be protected by a safety porch, the door of which can be closed before the aviary door is opened. If not, a small (low) access door in the flight can be featured. It must be entered carefully so that birds do not fly past the owner and away.

A lovebird aviary cannot be planted because parrots quickly

Do not underestimate the power of the lovebird's beak when designing your aviary

destroy vegetation. However, artistic use of plants close to the aviary greatly improves its aesthetic appeal.

It is important that the aviary flight is sheltered from prolonged direct sunshine, and from heavy rain, wind and snow. This does not, however, mean under the overhanging branches of trees. These can present many problems.

The base of an aviary should ideally be of concrete to enable it to be easily hosed. Failing this,

slabs will work well. Even gravel is better than bare earth, which represents a considerable health hazard to the lovebirds.

MATERIALS

Although less costly, the use of wire netting is not recommended for aviaries. Weldmesh of at least 19 gauge and 2.5 x1.25 cm (1 x 0.5 in) hole size is recommended. This has good strength, does not readily sag, and will last almost a lifetime, especially if periodically coated with bitumen (but remove the birds until this is dry).

The framework for the flight should be at least 5 x 2.5 cm (2 x 1 in). It can be made into panels on which the weld mesh is stapled. Be sure the wood is protected from the beaks of these powerful little parrots. Thin aluminium sheeting will serve this purpose.

The shelter/bird room must be light and well ventilated, as both of these features have a tremendous affect on the health of the birds. Novices often underestimate this.

The environment you provide has a profound effect on the well-being of your lovebirds

5 Caring For Lovebirds

It is advisable to collect your new bird as early in the morning as possible. This allows it ample time to settle into its new home and explore during daylight hours. If it is a pet bird, do not allow children to unsettle it during this traumatic period in its life. The hand-reared or finger-tame youngster can be allowed on to your finger after an hour or two of becoming familiar with its new surroundings.

DANGERS

The rooms in a home may hold many dangers for a lovebird. Safeguard against these before allowing the bird freedom to fly or flutter around any of the rooms it is given free access to. The most common dangers are the following.

Windows: On the first occasion a bird is allowed out of its cage, it may instinctively head for what appears to be open air – the window. Be sure all of these are closed. The bird can badly injure or kill itself if it crashes into glass. Place netting or sheets over the windows and any large mirrors, or close window curtains or drapes to prevent this from happening.

Dangerous Objects: Chimneys and open fires without protective guards, radiant heat electric fires, aquariums without hoods, extractor and cooling fans, potentially poisonous indoor plants, open tins of paint or dangerous chemicals, electric tools and other pets such as dogs and cats.

Dangerous Rooms: The kitchen should be out of bounds to all pet birds because it holds so many dangers. Frying pans on a stove, pans with boiling water in them, boiling kettles, the stove hobs, sinks full of washing-up water, hot irons, sharp knives – and on it goes. Even the fumes from non-stick pans and cooking oils can be poisonous to a small bird. Bathrooms can also be potentially fatal if toilet seats are left open, or if the bird landed in a bath or sink of water and this went unnoticed by the owner.

FEEDING LOVEBIRDS

Lovebirds are very straightforward in their dietary needs, and so should present no problem to the hobbyist. This said, the old concept that parrots can subsist on a seed-only regimen is incorrect. They require fresh fruits, vegetables and other plant matter, as well as a few items of animal origin, which provide certain proteins that cannot be obtained from plant foods.

It is true that these and all other parrots can survive on a spartan diet, but the object of aviculture is to maintain peak health and breeding vigour in birds. This cannot be done on diets lacking

A balanced diet is essential in order to maintain peak health and breeding vigour.

balance. It is one of the prime reasons breeders of past years struggled to establish long-term breeding populations in some species.

BALANCED DIET

It is not sufficient that a bird has adequate quantities of food. It must receive these in such a way that, collectively, they provide the necessary constituents enabling all bodily systems to function to their maximum efficiency. An all-seed diet will enable a bird to live, but it will be deprived of certain vital amino acids, vitamins and minerals. Eventually, these omissions will result in a lowered resistance to disease, a shorter life span, reduced breeding ability, poorer than normal eyesight, inferior feather quality and so on. The more varied the diet, the less chance there is of anything being missing. Supplying the right constituents in the correct ratios is what hobbyists strive to achieve by study and observation of their birds.

SEEDS

Seed provides the staple part of a lovebird's diet. These food items can be divided between those that are very rich in carbohydrates, and those that have a high protein and fat content, with much lower levels of carbohydrates. The two main carbohydrate-rich seeds are canary and millet, of which there are numerous varieties. Cereal crops, such as oats, maize and corn, are other seeds within this group. The protein/fat-rich seeds include sunflower (striped is the most popular of the three varieties), hemp, maw, niger, safflower, linseed and pine nut. There are of course many other seeds that are rich in protein/fat, as well as most nuts. The ones named are those most commonly stocked by pet stores.

For normal day-to-day activity, the adult bird needs a high

Seed provides the staple part of the diet.

percentage of carbohydrate foods, with other seeds supplied in smaller amounts. While growing, and when in a breeding state, extra amounts of protein and fat-rich seeds are required. Aviary birds will also appreciate somewhat more of the fat-rich seeds during the winter periods – they help to maintain adequate under-skin (subcutaneous) fat levels to insulate against the cold.

Always purchase the finest-quality seeds, as these are the most nutritious and the least likely to contain excessive dust. Never feed seed that has a split in its husk, from which oil is seeping. This is highly toxic. Store seeds in a closed container within a cool, dry, dark and well-ventilated cupboard. Seed must always be available to your bird on a free-choice basis.

SEED RATIOS

If you keep only one or two pet birds, it is best to purchase ready-mixed seeds as sold for small parakeets or parrots. The breeder will find it more economical to purchase individual seed varieties and make up their own mixture. As a basic guide, this should contain 50 per cent canary, 40 per cent millet and 10 per cent protein/fat seeds.

Millet is always a favourite, but it can lead to obesity.

All birds enjoy millet sprays (dry or soaked), but these should be rationed, or the bird will tend to glut on them and may become obese. Apart from this, they may spoil the appetite for other nutritionally important seeds and foods.

SOAKED SEEDS

These are especially nutritious and beneficial to young birds, breeding stock and those recovering from an illness. Soaking starts the germination process and changes the nutrient values – the protein and vitamin quantities increase. Such seeds are also easier to digest. Seeds soaked long enough to produce small shoots are actually the most beneficial, but they must smell fresh and display no signs of mould.

A small quantity should be placed in a shallow dish in a warm, dark cupboard. After 24 to 30 hours the seeds should be thoroughly rinsed and given to the birds. Soaked seeds have a short exposure life and may quickly attract bacteria and moulds. It is essential that any uneaten after a few hours are removed and discarded.

GREEN FOODS

Under this heading, we can include all fresh plant foods – fruits, vegetables and wild plants. These, especially fruits, are rich in vital vitamins and important trace elements – iron, copper, magnesium, selenium and others. The amount of these foods that birds will eat varies considerably, as does their individual palate for different items.

The fruit range includes apples, grapes, oranges, strawberries,

apricots, bananas, kiwis, pineapples, raisins, fresh figs – indeed, any fruit you are likely to eat – but avoid avocado, which is reputed to be harmful (I never did try this, on the sound basis of 'if in doubt, leave it out'). Vegetables include carrots, boiled potato, beans, peas, spinach, beets, kale, lentils and watercress, as just a few examples.

Wild plants enjoyed by birds include dandelion, parsley, thistle, chickweed, the heads of seeding grasses and groundsel. Branches and twigs of fruit trees, hawthorn, willow and any others known to be non-poisonous are essential food items. All fresh foods should be rinsed before being fed to the birds. Never feed any plant grown from a bulb.

OTHER FOODS

There are many foods of non-plant origin that are valuable to lovebirds for the proteins they contain. Among these are boiled egg yolk, cheese, small slivers of meat, honey, milk in small quantities (soaked into bread), beef extracts and fish liver oils.

Pellet foods are very popular with some owners, and disliked by others. While I would never feed pellets, as some do, as the staple

A balanced diet is essential in order to maintain peak health and breeding vigour.

diet of a lovebird, they are useful supplements in small quantities. Beware of any promotions that claim this or that product meets all the dietary needs of your birds. The fact that 'new and improved' formulas are always being bandied about suggests to me the previous formulas left something to be desired!

All fresh foods have short exposure lives and so should be fed in small quantities. Those uneaten after a few hours must be removed and discarded.

JUNK FOODS

Never feed food items that offer no nutritional benefit. Among these are sweets (candies), chocolate, sweet biscuits (cookies), crisps (potato chips), fried potatoes (hash browns), alcohol, salted peanuts, popcorn and their like. Not only do they offer no value to the bird, but they can also satiate part of its appetite so it eats less of the foods that it really needs. It can be difficult to persuade a bird to eat certain healthy foods, so letting it eat junk

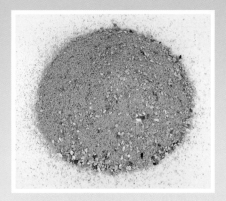

A supply of grit must always be available.

Crushed charcoal can reduce the risk of digestive upsets.

Cuttlefish bone is a rich source of calcium.

foods merely complicates this process.

GRIT AND MINERALS

It cannot be overstressed that all seed-eating birds require grit in order to be able to digest seeds and other solid foods. It must be available to them at all times, and it must be of the necessary sharpness and size. Within the gizzard, it helps to break down the food and prevents it becoming lumpy. Eventually, the grit becomes worn and is expelled from the body in the faecal matter after valuable minerals have been extracted from it.

Purchase the grit that is sold for small parrots. The addition of some crushed charcoal is also helpful in reducing the potential for digestive upsets. Cuttlefish bone is another valuable item, rich in calcium, and can be clipped to the cage bars. Oyster and eggshell are other sources of grit and minerals.

SUPPLEMENTS

There are many tonics and dietary supplements produced these days. They are marketed to play on the owner's fear that something may be missing in the bird's diet, which the supplement will provide. While this may be true, it may equally not be so. To feed certain supplements can prove as dangerous as it could be beneficial, this being especially so with respect to vitamins and minerals.

If your bird consumes a wide-ranging diet that includes seeds and green foods, and it displays no signs of ill health, it is unlikely to benefit from random feeding of tonic supplements. These should only ever be given to provide an ingredient missing in the diet. This is best determined after consultation with your vet, who will suggest the specific supplement needed. The indiscriminate use of supplements – and medicines – can be extremely dangerous.

FEEDING METHOD

When you obtain your lovebird, its former diet should be maintained even if changes are deemed desirable. Let it overcome the trauma of the move first. Dietary changes should always be effected on a gradual basis, spread over two or more weeks. If a bird has been fed on a seed-only diet, or one that included little green food, care must be exercised in suddenly feeding green foods (meaning all fresh foods).

Introduce them in small amounts so that the bird's digestive system can develop the flora needed to synthesise them efficiently. If any item is added in a glut, the result will be a digestive upset, which could weaken the bird's immune system and create more serious problems. Green foods are best supplied in the early morning or late afternoon, especially to aviary birds, where the heat of the afternoon sun will speed up their deterioration.

Feed staple seeds in one dish and optional seeds (high protein/fat) in another, or even in two others. This creates less wastage because birds will tend to throw out the less favoured seeds. Fresh foods can be hung on clips from the cage or aviary wire, or

If you use a seed-dispenser, check daily to ensure there is no blockage.

risk of a blockage. Open pot dishes should have the husks blown away daily to ensure there is seed in the pot, not just empty husks.

NEW ITEMS
Every lovebird is an individual and may not partake of foods the book says are good for it. Apart from familiarity of taste, you should not overlook the fact that sight is also very important to your bird. If an item is unfamiliar, it will often be ignored. Do not withhold an item just because it was ignored on a few occasions.

You can try two different approaches. One is to mix small quantities of the new item with those the bird likes – for instance, a few new seeds can be pressed into a fruit. The second method is to withhold a favoured item and introduce the new one. However, do not withhold staple foods for longer than a few hours – just long enough to encourage the bird to try the new food.

Some birds can be extremely stubborn, and steadfastly refuse to try foods known, by the owner, to be beneficial. In such instances you must use all your ingenuity, without actually ever denying the bird its needed rations.

fed in a pot feeder, according to the food item.

When using automatic seed dispensers, be sure to tap these each day to make sure there is no blockage. Those with wide receiving trays are better than the narrow ones because there is less

Some birds may be stubborn about trying new items introduced to the diet.

Water must always be available, and it must always be fresh. Exercise caution when thinking of adding medicines or tonics to water. It may change the taste and the bird may refuse to drink, which is counterproductive. Apart from this, it is an unreliable means of administering any additive.

ROUTINE CARE

WING CLIPPING

When the wings of a bird are clipped it is unable to gain height and quickly flutters to the floor or other landing area. The extent of clipping determines how much height the bird can gain. Some owners dislike this practice, others find it beneficial, especially with birds not fully finger-tame. Provided the clipping is effected correctly, and the feathers of each wing are trimmed to the same length, the advantages outweigh the negatives for a newly acquired pet bird. The pet will more rapidly accept and depend on the owner moving it from one place to another.

If the bird cannot gain full height it will not perch out of reach, nor gain sufficient height and speed to crash into glass windows or mirrors. It will be much easier to catch, because most times it will land at a low point. Should it escape outdoors, it will not go far, and so can be recovered.

The negatives are that, if it escapes and this goes unnoticed, its chances of avoiding dogs and cats are virtually nil. If other pets are in the home, especially cats, it may quickly be pounced on. Also, it will more readily land on dangerous objects, because it cannot control its flight as normal. If clipping is the chosen option, have an experienced person show you how to do it. Never trim the feathers of one wing only, as this results in a curved flight; this is psychologically damaging to the bird.

For neatness, the outer two primary flights should be left intact. Alternate feathers can also be clipped, and the trimmed feathers will not be noticeable. Clipped feathers will be shed and replaced at the next moult. If, by then, the bird is very tame, it can be given its full flight capacity.

CLEANING

It cannot be overemphasised how important daily cage cleaning is.

Many problems that are encountered by owners stem from not attending to this. Each day, the floor tray must be cleaned and all cage bars wiped. Perches should be rotated on a regular basis so they can be thoroughly washed in a dilute solution of disinfectant, then rinsed and dried.

Birds continually wipe their beaks on both the bars and the perches, and this is how bacteria and parasites gain entry to their respiratory system. Open food and water pots should be washed daily.

OBSERVATION

The more you observe your lovebird, the more rapidly you will be aware when some aspect of its appearance or behaviour is not as normal. This may be the first, indeed the only, indication of a health problem. It is especially important you stay near the cage at feeding times to become familiar with which foods it eats first – these will be its favourites. You should also know how much, on average, it drinks over a two-day period. Observe its faecal matter for colour and viscosity changes.

Both the beak and the claws should be inspected on a regular basis so they can receive veterinary

It is essential to keep a close check on all birds so you can detect any signs of ill health at an early stage.

attention in the event they become overgrown. This will not normally be the case, unless the bird is being fed an incorrect diet, lacks satisfactory perching, or has a genetic or other disorder causing the problem.

OUTDOORS

On warm spring and autumn days, a caged lovebird will enjoy the feel of fresh air on its body. The cage must be placed in a safe location where cats will not be able to frighten it. It must also be sited where the bird will not be subjected to long hours of direct sunshine that it cannot escape from.

A small outdoor flight would be ideal, because if there happened to be a light rain shower, the pet would enjoy this. Part of the flight should have a protective roof cover that the bird can retreat under when it wishes.

HANDLING

There are two things that the novice should be aware of. Firstly, if you want your lovebird to step on to your finger, you must position it so that the pet can step upwards. Parrots will not step downwards. Secondly, it is important that the bird does not have to reach for the finger. If it does, it will do so by using its beak to take a hold before bringing up a leg to grasp the finger. So, place your finger close to the bird, and at lower than chest level.

Should you need to inspect your pet, it must be grasped so that your hand encircles its back. The thumb and index finger must be placed on either side of its lower cheeks. If the head is not secured in this manner, it will have the opportunity to turn its head and inflict a painful bite on your finger or thumb.

TRAINING

Lovebirds have been taught to talk, but they are not gifted in this area. Training is best done in the evening when the bird is drowsy and will focus its attention on you. There must be no other distractions in the room – people, TV, or other pets. Simple repetition of single words is the way to teach. It requires a great deal of patience.

Other aspects of training are more productive with these birds, who are natural climbers, and comical in their behaviour. The key to success is that a strong bond of affection must first be established with the bird. From this, all else develops quite naturally.

6 Breeding

Lovebirds are easy to breed. You will hear and read this often enough, and, up to a point, it is true of a number of the species. However, it must be qualified by saying 'providing the conditions and the birds are conducive to breeding'.

This immediately suggests that merely placing lovebirds together may not result in a clutch of healthy chicks. The fact is that even the most experienced breeders, with the most popular species, can experience failures in spite of all their know-how.

The first advice is, therefore, not to take anything for granted about breeding these birds. If you do, you greatly increase the possibility that something will go wrong. For the female in particular, breeding is not only a very physically demanding process, but one that also creates high stress levels.

The relatively low cost of many lovebirds bears testimony to the fact that these birds will consistently multiply their numbers. What is not always appreciated is that, each year, many thousands of eggs fail to hatch, chicks fail to survive, and countless hens die during the breeding process.

A large percentage of these deaths could have been avoided. They are experienced by beginners who had read that 'lovebirds are easy to breed'.

In this chapter, the emphasis is on how to start correctly, and what can go wrong. You are recommended to follow up this text with much more detailed study of the subject before you actually proceed with practical breeding. By so doing, you will increase your chances of success, and reduce the possibility that life forms will perish due to impatience and lack of knowledge.

BE PREPARED

Before breeding stock is obtained, prepare their accommodation and the furnishings needed. An outdoor aviary is really the best way to commence, because it will result in fitter and hardier stock. The number of potential problems, especially with regards to egg development, will be reduced.

However, if indoor breeding is to be attempted, the minimum need should be a roomy indoor flight with measurements of about 1.5 x 1.5 x 1.2 m (5 x 5 x 4 ft). The beginner is ill advised to think in terms of cage breeding. It has been the source of many problems with popular foreign birds. One, but preferably two, nestboxes will be required. These are discussed shortly.

Each breeding pair should have its own flight. You are not advised to attempt colony breeding until you have more experience and suitably large aviaries are available. Even then, colony breeding has limited benefits and has not a single virtue if you plan to produce exhibition-quality stock, or breeding stock worthy of being sold as such. Roomy stock cages will be needed for the weaned youngsters. Be sure there are more than sufficient food and water vessels on hand as replacements when others are cracked or chipped.

The beginner is not advised to attempt hand-rearing chicks by intent. The subject is too complex to be discussed in this text. However, hand-rearing may become an emergency necessity, so it is prudent to have the necessary equipment on hand. Consult a detailed book on this subject.

Finally, you are advised to join your local and/or national lovebird or parrot society.

Apart from receiving their very informative newsletters, you will have access to many hobbyists who have a lifetime's experience with these birds. The newsletters provide a place to advertise your future surplus stock – especially if it is of a quality type.

NESTBOXES

These can be purchased from avicultural suppliers or home-made. Lovebirds will accept a range of sizes and styles. A key aspect is that they should be made of substantial timber so they will retain humidity, as well as provide good insulation against the weather.

A typical size will be 15 x 15 x

The nestbox should be made of substantial timber.

23 cm tall (6 x 6 x 9 in) and made of 1.25 cm (0.5 in) timber. It should contain a 5 cm (2 in) diameter entrance hole just below the roof, and a landing perch beneath the hole. A side or rear hinged inspection door situated just below half the height distance is useful, and preferred by some to the hinged lid type.

A false floor in the form of a removable piece of timber placed in the bottom of the nestbox will prolong its life. As it becomes worn, it can be replaced. A sloping roof with an overhang is useful if the box is sited within the flight and subject to becoming wet during showers. It is worth hanging two nestboxes up initially, at different locations, so the hen can choose the one she prefers. Sometimes the location of a nestbox can make the difference between birds going to nest or not.

A final point is that some breeders leave nestboxes in place all year round, in which case the birds will use them all year round to roost in. However, the pair may then also breed all year round. This is not advisable and can result in problems for the hen and chicks

SEXING LOVEBIRDS
Generally, the female will perch with her feet set wider apart than the male.

Male.

Female.

birds take no great interest in the nestboxes (other than for roosting), you probably have two cocks.

BREEDING AGE

Lovebirds are physically mature when about one year old. Breeding before this age is not recommended. Once old enough, the next thing is to ensure that they are in the peak of good health. Never attempt breeding if one of a pair is ill or recovering from an illness, or is obese or thin – especially the hen. Spring is the best time to commence, because the days are getting warmer and longer.

Under artificial conditions, lovebirds will breed all year round and require a light/dark cycle of 12/12 hours, which equates to the cycle of their wild African homelands. Once adult, these birds will produce chicks for a number of years, though the clutch size will dwindle as the birds get older.

BREEDING FACTS
Once a pair of birds has mated, the eggs are usually laid about ten days later. The clutch size is typically four to six eggs, but up to eight could be laid. The hen will incubate these for a period of 21 to 24 days. The white eggs are laid on alternate days and the hen normally begins incubating in earnest after the second or third egg is laid. During this period, the cock will feed the hen and periodically sit with her.

The chicks are weaned when about six weeks old, but will continue to be fed by the male for about another week. After this, they should be removed to a stock cage and are normally ready to go to new homes when eight weeks old. It is probable that the female will lay another round of eggs before the first chicks are weaned. Throughout the breeding period, it is essential that the birds are given quality foods, and extra rations once chicks are present.

PROBLEMS
There are many things that can go wrong when lovebirds are bred.

Among these are egg-binding (the hen is unable to pass an egg); abandonment of eggs or chicks due to mite infestation of the nestbox; cannibalism of the eggs or chicks; non-fertilisation of eggs; eggs that are soft-shelled; eggs that are thick-shelled, so the chicks die in the shell; chicks that die because they are not strong enough to break through the shell; and mis-shaped eggs.

In most instances, the source of the problem will be lack of hygiene, unfit breeding condition, inadequate diet, poor parental stock, or incorrect humidity within the nestbox (usually, the air is too dry). In the case of incorrect humidity, birds bred indoors are at greater risk than aviary-bred birds. Be sure the parents have an adequate bathing facility and fresh green twigs.

LEG RINGS
Closed or split leg rings are placed on one leg of the bird to serve as a means of identification. Only metal rings (not the plastic varieties) will survive a lovebird's beak, and stainless steel is preferred to aluminium. The closed ring is year-dated and can carry a breeder's number. Rings are obtained from specialist

A clutch of newly-laid eggs.

The eggs are incubated by the hen for a period of twenty-one days before hatching.

The chicks are born naked, blind and completely helpless.

Two weeks old, and the change is dramatic.

By six weeks the lovebirds are ready to leave the nest.

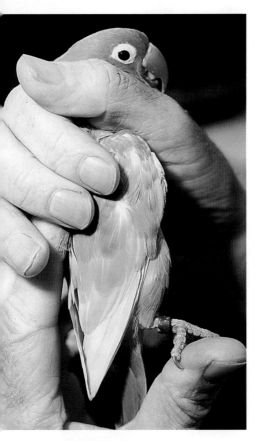

*Leg rings are used as
a means of identification.*

instances, the ring must be removed by the vet before permanent damage is caused. Hens may throw ringed chicks out of the nest, or injure the chick in attempts to remove the ring. The ring is placed on the leg when chicks are about five to eight days old, and fitting instructions are supplied with the rings.

EXHIBITION

For many breeders, the bird show is the prime reason they are breeders. They enjoy the competitive atmosphere and the many friends they make. It is a very social gathering, but one that is also very demanding, time-consuming and costly. Lovebirds are not 'natural' show birds, and so require much more training than many other foreign birds, otherwise they will simply crouch in a corner.

manufacturers (who advertise in avicultural magazines) and must be of the correct size for lovebirds.

Not all breeders will use them, because they are not without potential problems. Debris may clog between the leg and the ring and cause swellings. In such

However, once a breeder has established a reputation as an exhibition breeder, his or her stock will usually be in good demand. All potential breeders should visit shows because it is the one place where quality stock will be on view. It is the shop window to the entire avicultural hobby.

7 Health Care

An ounce of prevention is worth a pound of cure. The truth of this old adage should never be underestimated. Unfortunately, it often is, and for a number of reasons. In the case of the pet owner, it is invariably a combination of lack of knowledge and neglect. For breeders and dealers, it will be due to lack of time, space, cash and sadly, in some instances, because of neglect due to a lack of concern for the birds. They are merely a means of making money.

Even those who maintain the highest of husbandry standards are not exempt from disease; total eradication of pathogens can never be achieved.

It is a case of constantly taking those precautions that will keep them to the lowest level of incidence, and so less likely to be able to proliferate in the sort of numbers that will overcome the immune system of the bird.

'Constantly' is the key word – it is relaxing of standards that gives pathogens the time needed to multiply.

Another major problem, especially with pet owners, is that they seek simple answers and cures for what may be highly complex illnesses or conditions. As a consequence, they lose precious time by attempting home diagnosis and treatment on the advice of so-called expert friends.

Many physical signs of illness could be indicative of a whole range of problems. Microscopy and faecal/blood analysis are often the only ways a diagnosis, and treatment based on this, can be effected.

With these facts in mind, this chapter is devoted to preventative strategy, and how you should react to problems when they arise. Leave diagnosis and treatment to your vet for all but the simplest ailments.

GENERAL STRATEGY

It is most important that your bird's diet is balanced, and that its living environment is always maintained in a clean state. Whatever else may be ignored, these two areas should never be neglected. For breeders, if time is a problem, the remedy is to reduce the number of birds kept, no matter how much of a hard decision this will be.

The same applies if space is limited and cages are being stacked where you would normally not place them. Overcrowding is a very real source of health problems, but it can develop on a gradual basis. Many a breeder has had their stock wiped out because of a sudden epidemic. Do not wait until a crisis happens – take steps to avoid it.

KNOW YOUR BIRDS

Assuming all is well with the environment and diet, the next need is to be aware, at the earliest time, if a bird has become ill. This is only possible if the bird is being observed every day, and every time you pass its cage. You must be familiar with the mannerisms, state of faecal matter, and eating habits of every bird in your collection. Only then will you be aware if any are not displaying normal behaviour.

SIGNS OF ILL HEALTH

Birds will generally display a problem via two means, either separately or in conjunction. These are physical signs and behavioural signs. However, sometimes, a bird may die without exhibiting any signs of a problem. In such instances, especially for breeders, an autopsy should be conducted via the vet. The cost is well worth it if it pinpoints a problem that can be overcome, and which may save others in the collection from contracting the same malady.

PHYSICAL SIGNS

Weeping, sunken, closed, half-closed or cloudy eyes; swollen nostrils; flaky skin; raised leg scales; bald patches; excessive loss of feathers; dry or constantly ruffled feathers; loss of weight; staining of the vent area; very watery (white) or blood-streaked faecal matter; mucous discharge from the beak; noisy or wheezy breathing; pumping action of the tail; lumps or abrasions; vomiting; or any indication of a damaged leg, beak, wing or tail. When two or more signs are displayed together, the problem is more serious.

ABNORMAL BEHAVIOUR

Lack of interest in feeding or drinking; excessive drinking; reluctance to perch; sleeping in an abnormal manner, meaning standing on both legs with head forward. Normally a bird sleeps on one leg with head turned and placed in the feathers of the nape of the neck, though young birds may be seen perched on both legs when resting.

Further signs are unwillingness

to be handled as normal; feather plucking (other than hens during the breeding period); straining to pass faecal matter or an egg; crouching in a corner of the cage; or sudden erratic and uncontrollable muscle actions.

ASSESS THE SITUATION

How quickly you respond to the signs of an illness can make the difference between life and death, and between eradicating the problem or giving it the time to become much worse and more widespread. Minor problems, such as chills or wounds, can become the precursor of major diseases if secondary infections set in due to the minor problem not being treated.

The signs and the general state of the bird will dictate how you react. If the signs are those such as flaky facial encrustation, excessive scratching or dry feathers, it is unlikely that the bird will rapidly die. Signs such as excess weeping of the eyes, any form of mucus, respiratory problems, or a hen straining to pass an egg, are much more serious and could be life-threatening within hours.

You must assess the seriousness of the situation and proceed accordingly. If in doubt, do not wait to see if things get better over the next few hours. Rather, contact the vet and relate your concerns. The vet will advise you if the situation needs immediate

attention, or otherwise advise you of the best course of action.

WHAT TO DO

The following are the various steps that should be taken once you are satisfied a bird has a problem. In all instances, other than for wounds or damaged limbs or beak, it should be assumed that all birds in the home or bird room are at risk, or have already contracted the problem, even if they are not displaying signs of it.

Make Notes: First, detail the time of day and the current symptoms. The notes should be updated if things get worse, and the time that new physical or behavioural signs should be included; this information may be useful to the vet when contacted.

Gather Faecal Samples: Place these in a small plastic container and place this into the refrigerator if a visit to (or by) the vet cannot be made relatively quickly. Do not place them in the freezer compartment.

Isolate The Patient: The sooner a sick bird is removed from the vicinity of other birds – and pets – the better. The single pet may, however, remain in its cage and will be less likely to be stressed than if placed in a strange location.

Apply Warmth: The temperature needed to be effective with unwell birds is 85 to 90F (29 to 32C). This will often overcome most minor complaints. In the case of an egg-bound hen, this alone may help her expel the problem egg (but contact the vet as soon as such a hen is seen – she will normally leave the nest and be found distressed on the cage or aviary floor).

The best way to apply heat is with a dull emitter infrared lamp (bright lights are not helpful to sick birds). Every pet owner should own one of these. This should be placed on its stand at one end of the cage, a minimum of 15 cm (6 in) from the cage bars. This allows the bird to move away from the direct heat if it becomes uncomfortable. Two perches should be supplied, one at normal height and one low down for the very weak bird.

A thermometer outside, but near the cage, is needed to monitor the temperature. The

lamp, once on, should be kept on continuously until the bird is well, or until the vet advises otherwise. Remove soft and green foods, but never the water.

Check Other Birds And Conditions: Once the patient is removed and settled, all other birds should be carefully checked. It is a good time to review critically the environment and general cleanliness levels. Review feeding and the source of food, and think about how the problem may have gained access to your bird(s).

TREATMENTS

If the problem is an external parasite – mite, lice and the like – modern anti-parasitic drugs from your vet are highly effective. All birds should be treated and the premises thoroughly cleaned. Burn all perches and replace them. It is especially important that cage corners are given extra attention, for this is where many parasites hide during daylight hours. Other pets may have been the source of the problem, so must be checked and treated as well.

Internal parasites, such as worms and other pathogens, can

be treated with broad-spectrum drugs, but these tend to be less effective than species-specific treatments. These can only be used following identification of the species by the vet after faecal/blood microscopy and other means of analysis.

Medicines can be administered orally, topically (on the skin), via the water, or by injection. The last method is always risky with small birds because they may die of shock, so this is invariably a last resort. Water is a poor means of treatment because the bird may not drink enough to consume the correct dosage. Further, the medicine may rapidly loss efficacy if not drunk quickly.

WOUNDS OR BREAKS

Minor cuts should be gently wiped clean and a styptic agent applied. Once the blood flow stops, an antiseptic lotion or cream can be used. Do not attempt to dress such wounds, otherwise the bird will do more damage as it tries to remove this.

BIOLOGICAL DATA

Common name: Lovebird
Distribution: Africa, Madagascar
Genus: Agapornis
Number of species: 9.
Longevity: Approx. 10 years.

Recommeded breeding age:
12 months or older
Average clutch: 4-6
Incubation: 21-24 days
Weaning: Six weeks